Absurd

Foothills

Aidan Jones

ISBN: 978-1-0689112-0-0 (Paperback)
ISBN: 978-1-0689112-1-7 (Hardcover)
ISBN: 978-1-0689112-3-1 (Electronic Book)

Any references to historical events, real people, or real places are used fictitiously. Names, characters, and places are products of the author's imagination.

Front cover image by Ishani Gairola.
Book design by Aidan Jones.
Introduction image by Mondonna Pourjam.
Illustrations by Amy Black.
Edited by Calli Perry-Leslie.

Commercial usage rights for all artwork and illustrations have been granted to the author. All pieces remain under the ownership of the respective designers.

First printing edition 2024.

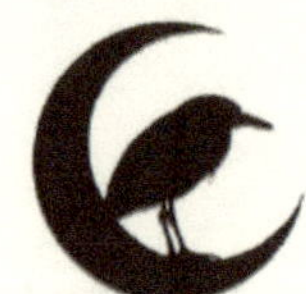

Little Heron Arts Collective
56A Mill St E
Unit #576
Acton, ON L7J 1H3

www.LittleHeronArtsCollective.com
www.AidanJonesOfficial.com

Dedications

This collection is dedicated to my father, who passed away earlier this year. Thank you for everything, truly.

I also want to thank my mom and my partner, who collectively make up just about the best support system a person could ask for.

And finally, a thank you to you for reading. This is one of the most special experiences a person like me could want, and I appreciate it more than I could ever put into words.

AIDAN JONES

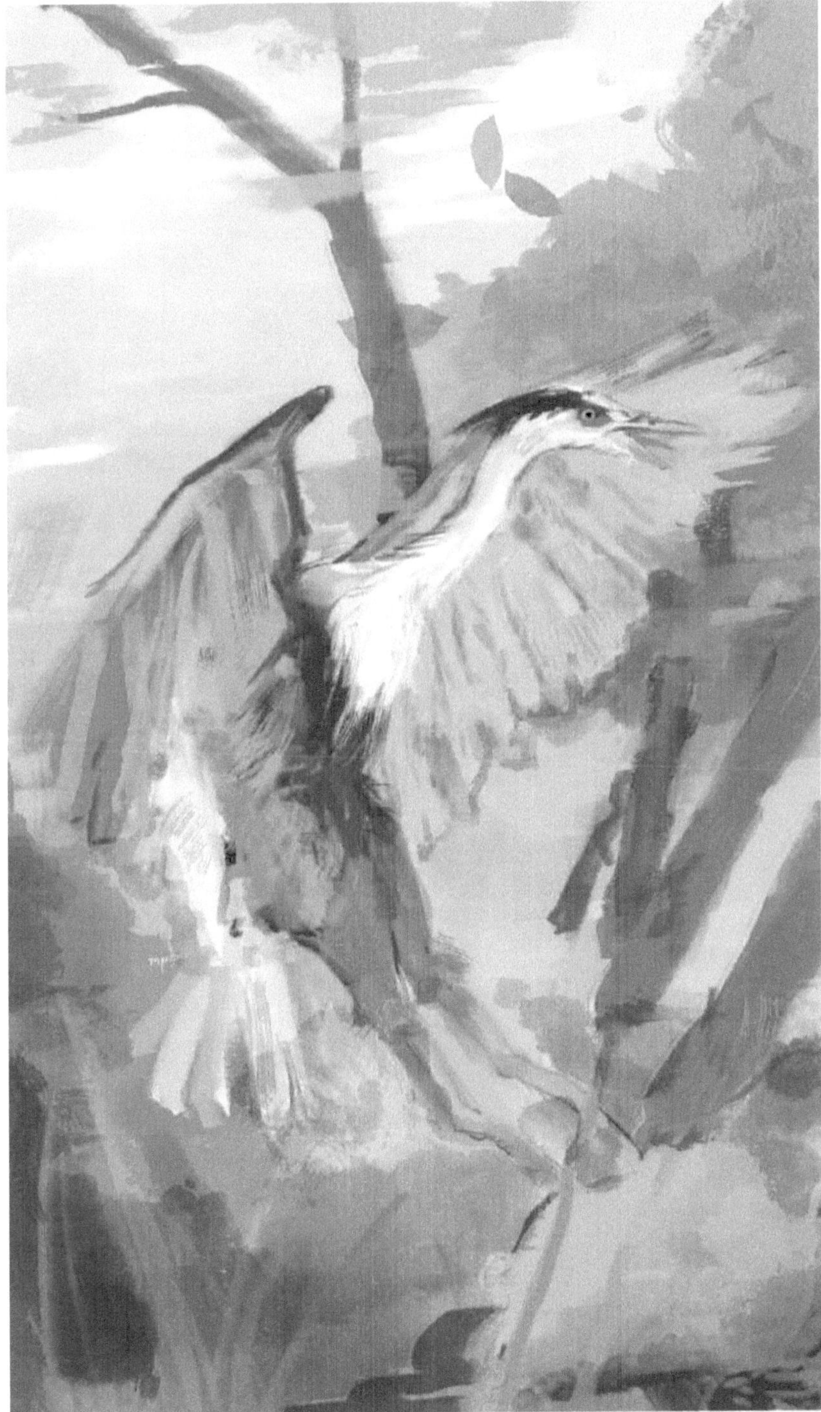

Contents

Introduction

Welcome to *Absurd Foothills*, a journey through the peaks and valleys of human experience, emotions, and introspection. In this collection, you will encounter a mosaic of existential poetry that explores the paradoxes and profundities of life, drawing from the raw beauty of nature and the intricate landscape of the human mind.

In *Absurd Foothills*, the reader is invited to wander through verses that capture moments of clarity amidst chaos and find solace in the familiar yet extraordinary contours of everyday existence. Each poem serves as a foothill, a chance to reflect on both the absurdity and wonder that coexist within our world.

This collection delves into themes of love, loss, hope, despair, freedom, and confinement. It examines the delicate balance between seeking meaning and embracing the unknown, guiding readers through an emotional terrain that is, at once, both challenging and comforting. These poems aim to explore the nature of humans' complicated relationships with intimacy, with family, and with the self.

The sporadic textures of this collection speak to the natural progression of feelings that I've experienced in the time that has elapsed since suddenly losing my father in early 2024. This work honours the messy, disjointed, and erratic process of grieving and healing, attempting to organize those emotions into three overarching mindsets that I have found myself shifting between over the course of the months in which I wrote the majority of these poems. Here, you will find an honest depiction of that experience, punctuated by reflections on a life that persists.

The title, *Absurd Foothills*, signifies the juxtaposition of the mundane and the magnificent. Just as foothills lead to towering mountains, the poems in this collection invite you to ascend from the simplicity of the familiar to the heights of introspection and revelation. Here, the absurdities of life are not just acknowledged but embraced, offering a unique perspective that encourages a deeper understanding of ourselves and the world around us.

Whether you find yourself at a crossroads or simply in need of a moment of quiet reflection, this collection promises a path worth exploring. It is a testament to the power of poetry to illuminate the human condition, transforming the ordinary into the extraordinary and the absurd into the profoundly meaningful.

Thank you for joining me on this journey. Enjoy.

— Part I —

Chasing Meaning

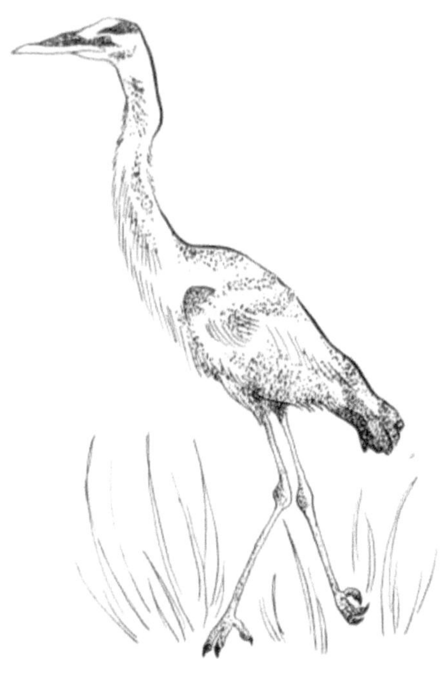

— *One* —

I chase meaning

In stories I've been told

About how this world is supposed to function

According to truths I've been sold.

There must be some reason

For this chain of events.

It's hard to accept

That destiny's gone cold.

— *Two* —

Six months have gone by

Since I saw you last,

Yet I still don't consider

You to be part of my past.

In my voice, I hear you,

In my actions and gestures,

Ingrained forever,

Alive and well in these letters.

— *Three* —

I dream of times that come, times that wait,

Times to derive hope from, even when destiny's late.

I dream of the daughter who asks if there's hope for her still.

I dream of the son who fights off demons with a pill.

I dream beyond the fence at the back of our yard,

The one I crawled under, never straying far

From the home that I knew,

The one that I broke,

The one that broke me,

The one that I took for granted,

When I chose to set myself free.

— *Four* —

Here and lost and there and found.

Meaning is thick until you're six feet underground.

For we all chase dreams that feel just right.

Because why start driving when there's no destination in sight?

— *Five* —

The gaze of the heron

That reminds those it meets

That the world of the beautiful

Is not quite so meek.

There's a power in beauty

That paralyzes the few

Who fly too close to divinity,

The sirens of pale azure-blue.

— *Six* —

The grapefruit on the counter went bad last night.

I could've thrown it out, but I'd grown fond of its sour smell.

Like a relationship that didn't sit quite right,

Sometimes there are feelings that logic alone cannot quell.

You complicate things, like a sticky, messy fruit,

But it's a fruit that I keep, because it reminds me of you.

— *Seven* —

I examine you.
I try to find meaning,
But this world is a place
Where order is fleeting,
Where truth is subjective,
And reason's completely
Devoid of progression,
Derailed discretely.
Criminals set free,
Families left weeping.
It's a system that's broken,
One that stops you from feeling,
Like there's an ounce of change to be had.

But I still hold on to hope,
Even if somewhat naively.

— *Eight* —

You are syllables, syntax, a collection of speech.

A storm of meaning and sounds keep your existence loud.

Open your mind, your words, please, teach me

What it is that lets you hear my silence in your crowd.

I remember the sound of you.

A memory of you still rings in my ear from when you meant

more.

A synonym for the one who occupied my mind's eye.

Memories of you echo inside from when loving you wasn't a

chore.

— *Nine* —

How far does the apple fall from the tree?

How much of who you were

Dictates who I'll be?

My actions, my thoughts…

Is my will really free?

I hear you in my voice,

A cadence that doesn't belong to me.

Maybe I exist as an echo,

A figure carved from your tree.

— *Ten* —

There's a moment in the fall,

When the sun beams through brown leaves.

Across the sky, dark clouds crawl,

Yet that light, still it finds me.

A chill air that holds

The hands of the few

Who kick around dampened leaves,

As autumn breezes blow through.

It calms a soul to its core

To feel the grip the gale wind streams have.

A season temperamental, yet aloof;

Oh, I regret how briefly you'll pass.

— *Eleven* —

Implicit to your search is knowledge

Of what lay beyond the bugs.

He won't come back.

What's gone is gone.

Yet nostalgia manipulates,

Forcing heartstring tugs.

— *Twelve* —

I dream of dandelion cotton mouth,

Sappy trees, and long-lost brown feathers.

Among the clouds, a lone bird flies from the south.

How I miss the chill of September sweater weather.

— Thirteen —

Coffee stream and autumn pipe dreams
Beg for me to consider coming clean.
Baited air waits for you to say you care,
But within a lie, I finally feel like I'm free.

What's a label if not a trick on the self?
Just another trophy to place on your shelf.
I heard there's compromise in definition.
"Is your goal just to live with yourself?"

— *Fourteen* —

I have climbed you before.

The view was grand,

The view was fleeting.

Tall, towering, taunting me with the fruits of my labour,

Yet I stand at the foot of you.

"With what arms, and what legs should I climb you?"

I'm stranded on Earth with no wings,

And the wingless crowd around me sings that same song,

"Oh where, oh where did our wings go?"

— *Fifteen* —

There needs to be harmony

Between the planned and the spontaneous;

They shape each other, doing their dance

Across the day-to-day of it all.

They'll trade who makes the first move.

— *Sixteen* —

Foothills house seeds of doubt and shame.

Those feelings given the power to pull my strings.

You tended to saplings of fear and became

The only one they trusted to speak their name.

When I'm standing under the tree,

Roots entangled throughout my frame,

I pray that light will shine through,

Heal on your pain.

You wanted to play, join in on their game,

But the tide is going out,

And in shallow waters,

We're all the same.

— *Seventeen* —

Silver strawberry tempest plays notes in your mind,
A feather of a child lost alone in the world shall not find
Any sliver of meaning that will help them to see
Beyond a shadow of a doubt what this world was meant to be.

She calls out from the mountaintop, perfectly free,
"Who am I? Who is me?"
Ahead of her lay years of torment, Oh she'll see,
But in those ails hails the person that she'll be.

— *Eighteen* —

Cross-stitch bones line my inner walls,

And pain is a reminder of he who has the gall

To paint a picture of a man so empty,

That even he who stares litters serenity.

— *Nineteen* —

Vinyl spins as patience thins.
We used to dance to songs like this.
I left you behind in spaces between the lines
Of lyrics you had tattooed on your wrist.

Our song is over,
It's come to a close.
A chapter finished,
Our melancholic prose.

I still hear that song from time to time,
But the nostalgia's no longer warm.
I still wonder if I crossed a line
Removing myself from the winds of your storm.

— *Twenty* —

In a field of tall grass

Where two lilac bushes bloomed,

You waited for me

To cure your early May gloom.

You asked me not to leave

Until you felt you had room

In your heart to accept

How I felt about you.

— *Twenty-One* —

Whiskey sour residue,

Coffee table rings.

Polish off that scuff,

Dad said leave no trace.

— Twenty-Two —

The raccoons in my neighbour's attic,

How young claws cut ladder rungs.

Thoughts find their way through noises erratic,

And I'm left to sort through stories unsung.

— *Twenty-Three* —

Put down your pride,

Put down your ego,

Put down your logic,

Put down your answers,

Put down your heartache,

Put down your jealousy,

Put down your labels,

Put down your guard,

Put down your defence,

Put down your ammo,

Put down your scripts,

Put down your narratives,

Put down your truth,

Put down your lies,

Put down that which holds you together at the seams,

And put down all else that clouds those eyes.

— Twenty-Four —

I don't know if you've heard but we're playing a game,

Where the rules ask you never to change.

"Please, please, just stay the same!"

Yet you contort yourself for fruitless fame.

There's no shame in trying to tame

Whatever it takes to give meaning to your name.

I feel like you'd know better than I do

What it would cost to clean this stain

Off a world from which you simply can't abstain.

Rumour has it you found a better way.

"Enjoy the game, take it day by day"

      You're starting to sound like one of them,

The victims who encourage an endless stay.

Colour draining, replaced with that grey.

      Who started this cycle that's turned me into prey?

— *Twenty-Five* —

Deathbed's doorstop taunts my final moment with you.

I never quite got to say goodbye.

So maybe I'll never know if it's true

What they say to those fated to die.

Whose face was the last to flash before your eyes?

"I miss you."

— Twenty-Six —

I carried to the curb the recliner that my dad slept in.

Hands piled on my shoulders as I wept for him.

"I can only imagine."

"Try to lift your chin."

There's a unique hell born in the feelings that I've been

Reeling from since you left me to stand for kin.

— *Twenty-Seven* —

I sleep in an idle town
Where misters and misses walk aimlessly down
This one path made of cobblestone
Hoping to see what's around.
Yet the town remains quiet and blue and so dreary,
Nobody can think and nobody can hear me
Speaking to them, they're in their own worlds,
But I really don't mind that I feel I'm alone.
Lately I've realized I might actually be prone
To finding situations where I'm left on my own.
It's easier to pause and simply stare at my phone,
In fact, I'm not even sure why I even left home?

I sleep and I dream,
But even in dreams my neighbours can't hear me.
I wonder if waking
Will finally set me free?

— Twenty-Eight —

The legacy that you left for me

Is one with expectations confused.

Sing me a song about the old acorn tree

And remind me of times when there was less for me to lose.

— *Twenty-Nine* —

There's something fulfilling
About chasing the thing
That fills you with light,
That which shrouds everything
Else in this world
With clouds of irrelevance.
"My all, I devote to you."
Tales of the pure and the innocent.

— *Thirty* —

You never had a chance

To see what would it be like

To follow through on your plans,

To find a future that fills you with light.

— *Thirty-One* —

Like a moth to the drywall,

You cling for eternity.

Plucked clean out of your element,

And swept up in modernity.

— Thirty-Two —

Long legs that separate lily pad banks,

Blanketed by dawn skies in a natural light.

Blue feathers dance on the water of the lake

As the eyes of the heron watch my paddle take flight.

— *Thirty-Three* —

They say you should never step on wildflowers,

But I didn't listen.

Stems crushed underfoot,

Thirteen blades of grass,

Crumpled and afflicted

By the weight of a giant,

A damaging fiend

Who didn't know better.

Lives touched, yet still strangers to me.

Petals folded by heels downturned,

A flower that housed a small ant

Carrying the carcass of a June bug

Back towards a mound of coarse sand.

Two bugs recently perished;

They met a similar fate.

It's not that I had ill intentions,

I was simply running late.

My attention was wandering.

I should've watched where I stepped.

Thirteen blades of grass,

Two bugs, and a stem.

Still, it's one foot after the other —

Oh, the weight of a June bug and an ant,

A tale born by that worse than fate,

And I feel I never quite paid my debt.

— Part II —

Losing Touch

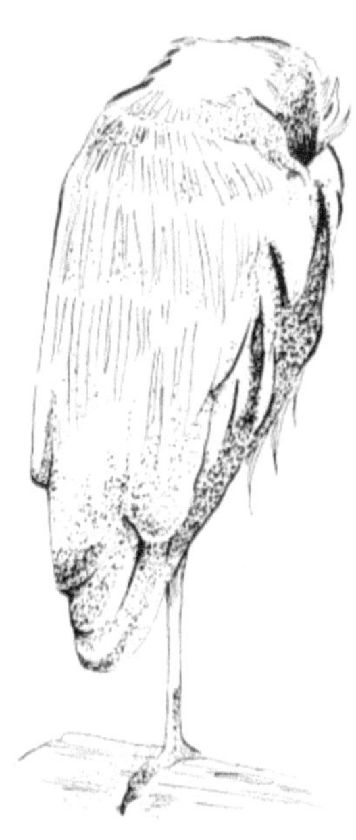

— *Thirty-Four* —

I fear I'm losing touch with that which held me strong,

A belief in something greater that kept me moving along.

I used to lean on order, in a frame that stood tall,

But the absurdity of life is setting in,

And I fear I may have been wrong.

— Thirty-Five —

I've lost touch with my senses,

I fear they've betrayed me.

Despite the trust that I've lent them,

My reserves of reason are running on empty.

— *Thirty-Six* —

I wasn't ready for you to leave.

How come nobody thought of asking me?

Feelings stripped bare by emotions so raw,

And now you're just gone, bandage ripped off clean.

Memories, regret,

At a part of me, they gnaw.

I'd prefer that you forget

And set your half of me free.

— Thirty-Seven —

I fear that I've lost you,

I worry it's been too long

Since I've felt you beside me.

Your presence feels so far.

It's not like I don't look,

I promise you I've tried,

But you drift further distant

With every day that wanders by.

— *Thirty-Eight* —

It's a balancing game,
Entrusting your name
To a person so different
Whose still in the frame.

You're part of me still,
Yet I feel I don't know you.
The person you became,
Like an echo from the past,
Dressed up all shiny and new.

— Thirty-Nine —

The absurd is naked.

It cares not for forgiveness.

In plain view, it asks you

If you've ever taken

A moment of your time

To really think through

What meaning is there here,

To decide what's false and what's true.

Right, wrong, and empty,

Plain, old, or new,

While we tend to our boulders,

Just like we've been taught to.

— *Forty* —

Peel your skin away, please, from that warm leather there.

It doesn't want you anymore

Discard your orange peel, dried in the midday sun.

It doesn't want you anymore.

Forget your directions to the coral shelf that lines blue water walls.

Nature can run introvert.

Strip yourself of whatever makes us burn,

Take some responsibility before someone gets hurt.

— *Forty-One* —

Your scratchy cotton sweater lays folded on the corner of my
mattress.
Memories of coarse fabric and pillow-top kisses distract me from
you.
Familiarity and our new normal replaced sweetheart shyness,
Who knew a heart could adjust to life without you?

— Forty-Two —

Trinkets remind me of a past me.

I'm nostalgic for him.

I feel the connection most in the morning.

Maybe moments after a fading dream crawls back to the recesses

of my mind.

My old clock sits in a box, ticking no longer.

It used to sing.

Not in any real way that most would enjoy,

But it sang to me.

He loved that clock.

I took the batteries out yesterday.

He noticed. I heard him cry about it.

Guilt feels like fire, doesn't it?

A swallowing force inside that grabs your heart and pulls.

"Grow up."

— Forty-Three —

What is a scar,

If not a reminder of war,

A battle once fought

Where skin keeps the score.

— *Forty-Four* —

Good morning, Dad.

Mom says she's seen you
In the eyes of the herons that fly by her house in the morning.
I'd like to say that I've seen you too,
But my hope of connection has faded since mourning.

I wanted to feel you, feel your presence out there.
But I'm met with thin air, the world's harshest blank stare.
I want to believe that you're somewhere, I do,
Yet I can't help but feel like my worst fear might be true.

— *Forty-Five* —

I've forgotten the feeling of making you proud.

Time's really passed since you've been around.

And I find the living room's gone quiet.

No sounds of coffee sipping

Or creaky wood board tapping.

Heavy midday breathing

Or dollar store pen scratching.

Sounds since silenced,

Because the living room's gone quiet.

— *Forty-Six* —

Struggle reminds those who've seen it.

It rears its head, and it cripples.

The scarred may remember,

It can be comfortable,

But the pain is stabbing.

It coaxes, and it tempts.

"It's your past."

"That's not you."

But it is still the old me

And we all get nostalgic.

— *Forty-Seven* —

"I want things to go back to normal."

Normal isn't fixed.

Normal isn't static.

Normal is a state.

It changes and morphs.

It follows us,

Swallowing each and every move of our lives,

Assimilating them.

The new normal.

The next normal.

Things will never be normal again.

— *Forty-Eight* —

Things feel heavier now

Without you around.

It's a different kind of pain

Than you'd feel after falling in the rain,

Or scraping your knee,

Or not getting enough sleep.

This kind of pain cuts too deep

And I feel like nobody truly prepared me.

— *Forty-Nine* —

Crush me under the touch of your tissue paper skin.

Remind me of that person who you've been,

Long before you took me for granted and made me miss

The taste, the push, the pull of that warm, unfaithful kiss.

— *Fifty* —

Grass-whistle tunes hum through empty city streets

While faint echoes bounce through the forest canopy.

I fear our bodies no longer touch under these linen sheets.

From end to end, charred embers have burned this tapestry.

— *Fifty-One* —

The man that I've become and I have a lot in common,

Except I don't know who looks through these eyes.

Never announcing his turn,

Causing mind, body, and spirit to cut familial ties.

— Fifty-Two —

Feelings hidden in the darkest crevices of an old me

That remembers the old you.

What happened to the old you?

Do you miss her like I do?

Do you mourn the loss of a kindred spirit

Who did her best to stay true

To all those who supported her, shouldered her, wouldn't leave

her side,

Like good friends are supposed to do?

But you're different now.

I guess it's true what they say, how

Birds of a feather only flock together

When the rain holds tight like glue.

— Fifty-Three —

I've lost your tracks and the storm is now lifting,

Howling winds hide that something in you is shifting.

What once was clear has become riddled with fear.

You know I love reminiscing on when your intentions were clear.

I'm not going to lie, I do feel betrayed

By this comfort you gave that I took to be mine.

And now we're left with the option to give things another try,

But you let your dreams of change chase us into the sky.

— *Fifty-Four* —

I've sunken down these last few days,

Yet the strings at my elbows keep my acting at bay.

It feels like a fabrication, a bit morally grey

To keep dancing this dance when I'd rather just stay

Inside and quit because this isn't my show.

"But hey, remember when you came up with those moves? The

rhythm? The flow?"

"What happened to the fire? The creative? The juice?"

Well, the fire went cold and the juice ran dry.

You think I wanted to keep chasing that high?

"Take some time, get out of your slump, just give it a try"

Yet I'm stuck here with strings on these damn elbows of mine.

— *Fifty-Five* —

I planted a seed a few years ago

And I hoped it would bloom into a better tomorrow.

Yet tomorrow came and went, and the soil never broke.

And now I'm left with vested interest in a pot of dirt,

A real sick joke.

— Fifty-Six —

I'll paint a picture of a time that hurt less.

I took a trip to the mountains, went hiking out west.

Times were simpler and waters a more vivid blue.

I didn't yet have to think what life would be like

If I had to do it without you.

— *Fifty-Seven* —

A new reality sinks into place

As I try not to let the distrust settle on my face.

But you're gone.

And I'm left to don the mantle of whoever you expected me to

be?

You're free, and I'm just me, again,

A few steps behind,

My brother and me,

Don't you see?

I'm sorry, I'm spiralling, this isn't me.

The pit in my stomach, it still gets heavy.

Can I have some water? A place to sit? Please.

Please, do me a favour, please just don't mind me.

— *Fifty-Eight* —

Are you proud of me?

Does it bother you that I

No longer pretend to be

A version of me

That is meant to placate family?

I am myself, a reminder of you somehow.

Yet no matter how hard I try, I still can't seem

To figure out how far my apple falls from your tree.

— Fifty-Nine —

Twelve feet separate action and reaction,
Between the two lay breaths of indecision.
A faint light inside is what remains of your passion,
Two steps forward, one step back, abandoning position.

The person you were, the person you knew.
They're long gone, replaced with someone who
Is familiar, yet may feel new to you,
Despite the feeling that I'm simply losing you.

— *Sixty* —

Salt in the wound of a fresh cut that sears as it is observed.

I thought about asking you for help that night,

But I didn't have the nerve.

You tried and you tried to work around my needs,

But my anxious thoughts and stomach knots left you without leads.

I've tried to let you in, I wanted help, I did,

But now I'm left wondering why I closed my doors to you,

My heart's melody is faint, a melancholic ballad.

— *Sixty-One* —

Vultures paint a picture opposite,

Black feathers and tight collar confident.

Leave me in the dark, circle him instead of me.

Bloody talons and crooked beaks that never set you free.

I've seen them in my dreams, birds of terror, birds of prey,

They haunt memories where fallen bodies lay.

The birds feed on what cannot be remembered,

Forgotten friends,

Mental dead-ends,

Down where falling-star wishes play forever.

— *Sixty-Two* —

It's not that I feel lost without you,

I still have a sense of where I am in this world.

It's more like a ship that's just lost its anchor,

Adrift with no answer to give the absurd.

— *Sixty-Three* —

Whiplash chases my dreams over absurd foothills.

Yet debt and rent and electricity bills

Keep my mind from straying too far away

From the "responsibilities" for which I still have to pay

To keep a roof and a bed and a pillow for me,

To rest and to sleep and to continue to dream.

Knolls so wide that dreams stack within them.

Petals and leaves that sprout from my stem.

Yet thorns sprout too, and from them, I bleed.

I can't help but think as I wipe the blood clean.

"Who would I be if not for those thorns?"

Those imperfections that make me into a storm

For anyone else who wishes to make my acquaintance.

I'm sorry if I hurt you, if you run out of patience.

I'd understand, truly, if I'm not your cup of tea,

But that's what you get without an umbrella near me.

— *Sixty-Four* —

Rhythmic push, humming pull

That consistent pressure against the sand

Cautious breeze, crashing careful

Foamy footprints where two lovers stand

Interlocking hands, chilled by ring-finger gold

"Let's start to head back, it's getting a bit cold."

— *Sixty-Five* —

I don't look for you

In the bottom of a glass.

Not my vice, not my truth,

Just a mistake of the past.

— *Sixty-Six* —

I found a home in the space between

The couch and you,

It was always enough for me.

Trapped in a space, a distant memory,

A past from which

I don't know if I want to be free.

— Part III —

Finding Peace

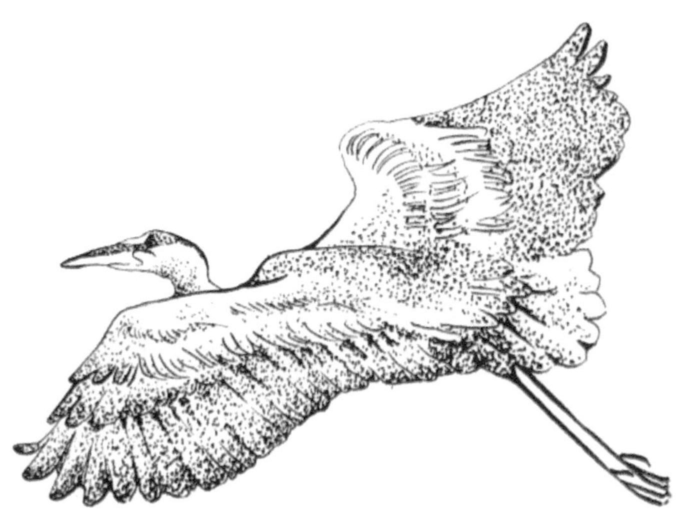

— *Sixty-Seven* —

In finding peace I realize

The errors of my ways,

Chasing meaning in a void

That hoped to lead me astray

From the truth, an absurd truth,

Among foothills that marked a pathless way,

Towards something I've lost touch with

In a world of blanketing grey.

— *Sixty-Eight* —

I am a collection

Of memories that sit just below the surface of my skin.

Black, inky murals that remind me of who and where I've been.

I am a collection

Of pains and griefs and solitudes.

Below my heart, those sentiments, they cluster and they seclude.

I am a collection

Of images and destinations that exist behind my eyelids.

Dreamlands that don't exist, but I promise, they're places I've

been.

I am a collection

Spaced perfectly between where I ought to and who I am.

For better or for worse, I was born a product of this land.

I collect and consist of.

I learn and then become.

I falter, but persist on.

— *Sixty-Nine* —

A wood grain collage,

Nature's mosaic display,

Oak tree mirage,

Where small infinities lay.

Leaves that have fallen here,

Now crushed beneath our weight

Remind me of those times

Before we had to confront fate.

— *Seventy* —

As light reflects

Off the slow-falling dust

That drifts from the rafters

And fills the space between us,

You tell me your dreams,

Your plans for old age,

Yet the story sounds familiar

Because our next page is the same.

— *Seventy-One* —

Bruises and spraying juices painting pebbles below.

Beautiful, sweet, picturesque, splattering mark.

You are now forgotten,

Damaged beyond repair,

Not fit to consume,

I leave you there,

To be someone else's treasure.

— *Seventy-Two* —

Black blade of grass,

Snow melts to show,

A dead wetted mass

Where the earth had drowned below.

It hides a dark past

That I hoped to forget.

It's where I saw you last.

Remember the night we both wept?

— *Seventy-Three* —

You were an untouchable feat,
Someone the child in me
Could never aspire to be,
So careless and free
With a bounce to your feet
But you made it look easy.

Yet I left and things changed,
I couldn't tell you when.
Two pieces that no longer fit,
But I like to think I've grown since then.

— *Seventy-Four* —

Opportunity presented itself today,

And in an unexpected form,

It offered me hope.

"Welcome home."

— *Seventy-Five* —

Blue heron wingbeats send soft gusts upwards.

I've always felt safer surrounded by the birds.

One day, I'll tell stories about the person that I've been,

A mental portrait, I'll give myself to you in words.

— *Seventy-Six* —

Ephemeral becomes your expression

As the shirt you wear is abandoned.

A hand on my chest, I comb through the thoughts

Of what lay just beyond my touch.

"Be impatient," you tell me from my side.

When to you my hands confide,

Your cheeks begin to blush.

Yet a stone from the garden shatters your round cocktail glass.

I reminisce on the pond of shattered light and pale brown

That's left behind while your mind chases you home.

A companion, a loan, alone.

— *Seventy-Seven* —

Candlelit panes separate thickening air.

You sit across, divided in space, but the room doesn't care.

Our arms are outstretched, but fingerprints leave grey on glass.

You speak, I speak, and always, the room speaks last.

I remember your head on my shoulder,

That honey-scented hair.

"I love you" and "I love you too" fill the heavy air.

Summer humidity, sweat-dropped brow, clouds overcast.

We won't speak of how our legs entangled

Crushed those innocent leaves of grass.

— *Seventy-Eight* —

There's a part of me that's forgotten
Exactly what it felt like to be hurt by you,
So instead I write and reminisce
On where I went wrong in handling you.

You know I don't resent you,
Yet it feels like I'm supposed to.
It drains me to stay so angry.
I wish I could just forgive you.

You put up your walls,
Hid behind them and threw
Daggers straight up and they'd fall
On anybody close to you.

Yet from behind that wall, you'd stand,
Unable to see the damage
You caused as we looked for shelter.
Even still, I don't resent you.

— *Seventy-Nine* —

I'm proud of myself, my work, and the person I'm becoming —
It finally feels like I can relax and stop running
From expectations and pressure and eyes looking down.
A mind in my skull and two feet on the ground.

There's a route that ends here with two white eyes,
Frigid, yes, but this is the road that I travelled by.

Beyond my mind exists a place I used to stay
Where the skyline was vibrant, without a sliver of grey.

— Eighty —

I look in the mirror and see *that* me.

That me who lacks responsibility.

He forgets sometimes to look after himself.

I know he'd rather just put me up on a shelf

And ignore who got this ball rolling where it needed to be.

Doesn't he understand that he should be thanking me?

Doesn't he know that I'm the cause

For all that we've got?

I worked past our flaws

And built something to be proud of for once.

I'm not running anymore from a reflection of me.

I don't mean to be blunt, but from myself,

I'm finally free.

— Eighty-One —

The horizon is a mouth that chews on daybreak.

It sips from small streams and swallows Great Lakes.

The trees become enveloped by that separating line.

What could have been one, land and sky must divide.

A gradient of hues, those opalescent blues,

They hold my attention, distracting me from you.

My thoughts roam to the man who calls the passing boat home.

Does the horizon make him think of his love too?

— Eighty-Two —

The morning mist spreads an inch above

The water that I know best.

From a distance, a monotone grey

Covers the canal ahead.

My paddle in the water draws circles,

Pushing me west,

Towards a future that makes more sense,

Out where the blue herons nest.

— *Eighty-Three* —

The absurd is a treasure.

We try to transform it,

Shape it and make it our own.

The absurd is glorious,

Yet trapped in a box.

Embrace it, live life on the edge, they say,

From the corner of their small office cubicles

Where they're forced to stay.

— Eighty-Four —

I betray a past me

By not caring about the things that once made me feel

A fire in my chest

Back when everything felt more real.

The feelings were honest,

They were me, and they were true,

But I've come a long way since then

And now I can be a better me for both me and you.

— *Eighty-Five* —

I held on to that sand,

Each and every grain,

But through my fingers, it slipped,

In the warm July rain.

Water soaked through my jacket.

I could feel it down to my knees.

Reminders of you and the words you've said

Are carried to me in the breeze.

— Eighty-Six —

I haven't forgotten the promise I made,

To make good on your effort, honour your pain,

To bring you back a reason to think,

That I meant what I said on that day,

I stayed true to who I said I'd be

Even if you're no longer here to see.

Each poem that I write to you

Is a foothill meant to convey a truth,

A promise, a secret, something I've learned

That I hope to share with you when I leave this Earth.

— *Eighty-Seven* —

The sun is setting on the words that brought you here.

I asked you to leave,

To give me space to breathe,

But you stuck around, held me close,

Always remaining sincere.

Emotions couldn't push you away,

The girl without fear.

And God, I'm grateful that you stayed

Here's to the rest of our years.

— Eighty-Eight —

Misty-eyed with tarnished pride,

You set back the healing I've been doing behind

The scenes while trying to bring back to you

A version of me, more authentic and more true.

I'm done with the lies, the pretending, the games

By the time that I'm done, there'll be no more shame.

My ultimate hope, my final claim

Will be to make you proud and lift up my frame.

"Stay close."

— Eighty-Nine —

This isn't a home.

It's barely got space

For the children to roam.

It's a room with three drawers,

Some storage under the stairs,

And a damn dent in the door,

But I suppose this is fair.

My bed folds in two.

The walls feel so bare.

Hands run from end to end smoothly

Except for that dent by the door,

And that screw coming loose,

But I've hardly a care

In the world now that pay is coming in.

I'll buy paintings for the walls

So my dent will blend in.

— Ninety —

A branch hanging downwards

From this trunk of mine.

Balancing, swinging

From me, you fly

Up, up, and away,

Into the sky.

Please become your own person

When you're no longer mine.

— Ninety-One —

"Well, what should I call you?"
See, it isn't that easy.
Sometimes I feel like a different person,
But my reputation precedes me.

There are layers to knowing me.
Well, not layers exactly,
Maybe a system of streams
That double-back and cross naturally.

They intersect in ways
That I find hard to describe.
One day I'm introverted
And the next, you'd see a different side.

I'd like to feel understood.
It warms the heart just to feel seen.
"Sorry, I'm bad at introductions."
I struggle to define me.

— Ninety-Two —

Milk froth shapes

Line coffee cup rims.

Chipped paint café mugs

Served by steam-blushed skin.

My rain jacket clings to me,

Soaked through thin,

As old rain droplets fall

On poetry book paper print.

Ink bleeds and it dries,

Taking new shape again.

Heads turn as thunder claps,

Just to see a fresh storm coming in.

— Ninety-Three —

A legacy disturbed by a stroke of poor timing.

That damn body you neglected

Has generated lessons that I'll heed

For years into the future,

Which for all isn't certain.

But yet I push onwards,

As time heals all burdens.

— Ninety-Four —

You've always been quiet.

Couldn't be something you can't be.

But in the end, you were trying

To be better for family.

I thought there was hope still

To heal the wounds that cut deep,

But in the end,

Time was waning,

So those memories I'll keep.

— Ninety-Five —

Brown sugar necklace,

A scent of crushed daffodil.

She hangs on to hope,

And her grip, it strengthens still.

— Ninety-Six —

I find it hard to listen to songs

That remind me of you,

But I don't think it's wrong

To need space to heal

From what made us bond,

You're a part of me still.

It hasn't been long

Since I heard your voice last,

And so long as I remember,

You'll never be gone,

Just a part of my past.

— *Ninety-Seven* —

An identity lost,

An identity that stays

Tucked away in a drawer,

Unallowed to play.

There are parts of me I hid

From the people outside.

They said they'd accept me,

But I assumed those were lies.

It was safer to pretend

That I wasn't me,

When someone would ask

Who I wanted to be.

A face in a crowd,

Easily forgotten,

Because standing out with pride

Felt like it would only lead to heartache.

I don't regret hiding.

It was a choice to feel safe,

But I do wish back then

I could've had that space.

— Ninety-Eight —

Was that you standing

In the cold January air?

I think this city holds grudges

Around this time of year.

Wind against my nose

That runs frigid as ice.

I'm happy to see you again

In these glowing streetlights.

— *Ninety-Nine* —

A transformation took place,

The dealer said, "Your identity may

Never go back to the way it was that day."

I agreed because I just can't stand to stay

In my mind any longer, I'm done

With feelings that encourage me to run

Away from myself as if I'm someone

That I should be afraid of. It's sad

To imagine that I'd feel the need to stand back.

Am I not proud of who I am?

Am I no longer Mama's little man?

Will she refuse to hold me tight and let me cry in her arms?

What's that? This race of ours is ending,

And I never stood a chance?

Just leave me in the dust,

It's fine, I never had plans

To compete. I'm just a man

With a confused soul and misguided hands

That seek to build a tower to plant my feet on and stand

Just a little taller with hopes of maybe reaching out to the stars,

And joining my dad up in the clouds where he watches me from
afar.

I cry as I write this because I fear he's not there.

In fact, I have dreams that he's actually nowhere,

Because he passed away a few months ago.

And really I worry that death is the end of something beautiful,

Not the start of something new.

Now I'm left here to pick up the pieces of a broken home

That misses you every single day that you're not here.

But I'm whole, you know, that glow didn't stop.

It definitely slowed, but I'm still whole.

I hope to see you again, I truly do,

But I've come to peace

With the fact that dream might not come true.

And you might be gone and that's just that.

I'll take care of Mom, I promise you that,

Not just her and I, but my brother too.

We'll do our best to turn this right around,

And take care of all that you left, while never forgetting you.

About the Author

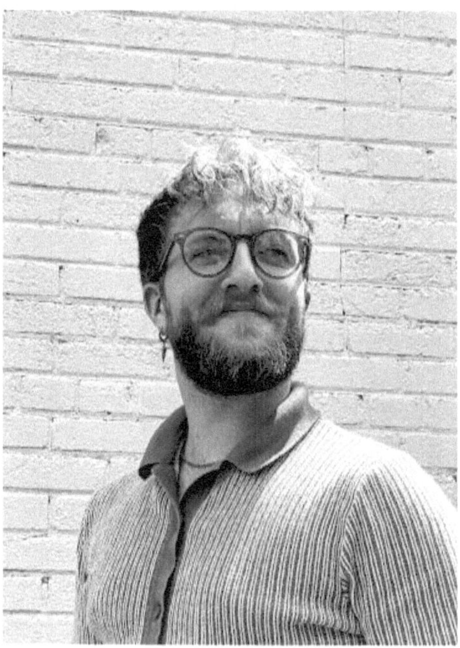

Aidan Jones is an emerging writer hailing from Ontario, Canada. His passion for the written word is matched by his love for nature, where he finds inspiration for his evocative and introspective poetry, as well as his numerous other creative endeavours.

An Honours BA graduate in English, currently pursuing a graduate certificate in technical writing, Aidan's work is marked by a deep appreciation for the nuances of language and the emotional landscapes it can convey.

When he's not writing, Aidan can often be found hiking through verdant trails, kayaking on serene waters, or capturing the beauty of the natural world through photography. His connection to nature not only fuels his creativity but also provides opportunity for escape from the daily ebbs and flows of a persisting life.

Aidan's poetry is a testament to his ability to weave the sublime with the everyday, creating a tapestry of words that resonate with readers after the last page is turned. Through his work, he invites readers to explore the depths of their own emotions and the world around them.

Thank you for reading. If you've enjoyed, consider lending this book to a friend.